GIANTS AND DEMONS

Mahishasura the Buffalo Demon

SHUBHA VILAS

Om Books International

The Demon King Rambha fell in love and married a buffalo. Soon, a son was born to them. Mahisha means buffalo and asura means demon, so the child came to be called Mahishasura.

Mahishasura was extremely powerful. However, he felt that despite their strength, his demon clan was a total failure. They were unable to conquer heaven. Mahishasura secretly desired to become the king of all the worlds.

Mahishasura knew that there was only way by which he could fulfil his desire. He would have to perform difficult and long tapasya and meditation. So, he stood on one foot under a tree for years and years.

Mahishasura stood in that posture for many years. Finally, Brahma appeared before him to grant a boon. Mahishasura said that he wanted to live forever and never die. Brahma refused. He did not have the power to grant that boon. Then Mahishasura asked for a boon that he should not be killed by any man or god. He was sure that a woman would never be able to kill him. Brahma agreed and granted him the boon.

Now there was no stopping Mahishasura. He attacked Earth. After much looting and destruction there, he attacked the capital of Heaven, Amravati. Vishnu, Brahma and Shiva all came together to save Indra's throne, but their combined forces also could not save them from the demon. Neither Vishnu's chakra not Indra's vajra had any impact on him. Mahishasura in the form of a buffalo, conquered the throne easily and the gods had to flee pathetically from their abodes to save their lives.

After many years of living out of heaven, the devatas gathered again to plan their way back. They knew that only a woman could kill the demon Mahishasura. Vishnu, Brahma and Shiva combined their energies and focussed intensely on creating a woman who would be invincible. Soon, a ball of fire appeared. Shiva gave it a face, Vishnu moulded the arms while Brahma shaped her legs.

They also equipped her with the chakra, trident and ganga water. All the gods then offered her gifts ranging from a red saree, to ornaments, to weapons like axe, bow and arrow, mace and thunderbolt. Finally, Himalaya, the god of mountains presented her with a vehicle, a tiger to ride on! She was named Durga and with their collective blessings, she set out on her mission.

When Mahishasura heard that a woman had come to challenge him, he scoffed. He believed himself to be invincible. What harm could a woman do? But he was wrong. Within moments, Durga destroyed his army by creating her own army. Alarmed, he changed his strategy and offered to marry her. Durga laughed and wounded him with her weapons. The battle went on for nine days.

Mahishasura turned into his buffalo form but Durga pounced on him and beheaded him with her chakra. That was the end of Mahishasura and his arrogant rule. Indra led the gods back to heaven and since then, Durga is worshipped for a period of nine days known as Navaratri.